This Recipe Notebook Belongs to:

Karl and Kristina

**For my husband and children,
thank you for enjoying my cooking everyday!**

BAKING INGREDIENTS CONVERSIONS

BUTTER

Cups	Grams
1/4 cup	57 grams
1/3 cup	76 grams
1/2 cup	113 grams
1 cup	227 grams

PACKED BROWN SUGAR

Cups	Grams	Ounces
1/4 cup	55 grams	1.9 oz
1/3 cup	73 grams	2.58 oz
1/2 cup	110 grams	3.88 oz
1 cup	220 grams	7.75 oz

ALL-PURPOSE FLOUR / CONFECTIONER'S SUGAR

Cups	Grams	Ounces
1/8 cup	16 grams	.563 oz
1/4 cup	32 grams	1.13 oz
1/3 cup	43 grams	1.5 oz
1/2 cup	64 grams	2.25 oz
2/3 cup	85 grams	3 oz
3/4 cup	96 grams	3.38 oz
1 cup	128 grams	4.5 oz

GRANULATED SUGAR

Cups	Grams	Ounces
2 tbsp	25 grams	.89 oz
1/4 cup	50 grams	1.78 oz
1/3 cup	67 grams	2.37 oz
1/2 cup	100 grams	3.55 oz
2/3 cup	134 grams	4.73 oz
3/4 cup	150 grams	5.3 oz
1 cup	201 grams	7.1 oz

CONVERSION CHART FOR THE KITCHEN

VOLUME MEASUREMENT CONVERSIONS

Cups	Tablespoons	Teaspoons	Milliliters
-	-	1 tsp	5 ml
1/16 cup	1 tbsp	3 tsp	15 ml
1/8 cup	2 tbsp	6 tsp	30 ml
1/4 cup	4 tbsp	12 tsp	60 ml
1/3 cup	5 1/3 tbsp	16 tsp	80 ml
1/2 cup	8 tbsp	24 tsp	120 ml
2/3 cup	10 2/3 tbsp	32 tsp	160 ml
3/4 cup	12 tbsp	36 tsp	180 ml
1 cup	16 tbsp	48 tsp	240 ml

1 GALLON =
4 quarts
8 pints
16 cups
128 ounces
3.8 liters

1 QUART =
2 pints
4 cups
32 ounces
950 ml

1 PINT =
2 cups
16 ounces
480 ml

1 CUP =
16 tbsp
8 ounces
240 ml

1/4 CUP =
4 tbsp
12 tsp
2 ounces
60 ml

1 TBSP =
3 tsp
1/2 ounces
15 ml

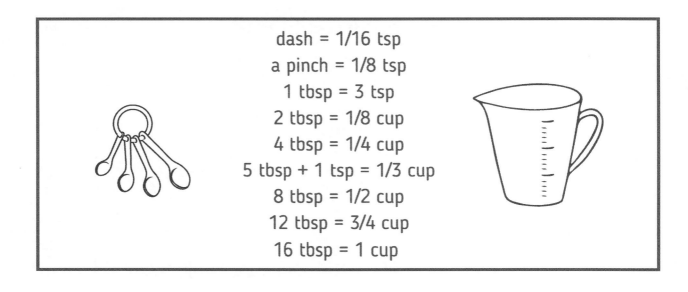

dash = 1/16 tsp
a pinch = 1/8 tsp
1 tbsp = 3 tsp
2 tbsp = 1/8 cup
4 tbsp = 1/4 cup
5 tbsp + 1 tsp = 1/3 cup
8 tbsp = 1/2 cup
12 tbsp = 3/4 cup
16 tbsp = 1 cup

OVEN TEMPERATURE FARENHEIT TO CELSIUS

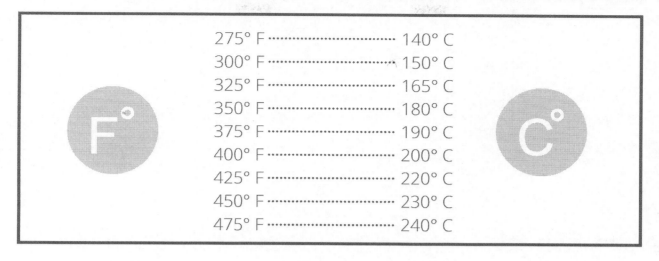

275° F ·· 140° C
300° F ·· 150° C
325° F ·· 165° C
350° F ·· 180° C
375° F ·· 190° C
400° F ·· 200° C
425° F ·· 220° C
450° F ·· 230° C
475° F ·· 240° C

SAFE COOKING MEAT TEMPERATURES

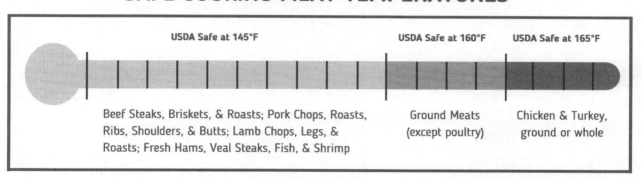

USDA Safe at 145°F

USDA Safe at 160°F

USDA Safe at 165°F

Beef Steaks, Briskets, & Roasts; Pork Chops, Roasts, Ribs, Shoulders, & Butts; Lamb Chops, Legs, & Roasts; Fresh Hams, Veal Steaks, Fish, & Shrimp

Ground Meats (except poultry)

Chicken & Turkey, ground or whole

COMMON INGREDIENTS SUBSTITUTIONS

BAKING POWDER
1 Teaspoon
1/2 tsp cream of tartar + 1/4 tsp baking soda

BAKING SODA
1 Teaspoon
2 tsp double-acting baking powder + replace acidic liquid ingredient in recipe with non-acidic liquid

BUTTERMILK
1 Cup
1 cup plain yogurt OR 1 tbsp lemon juice OR vinegar plus enough milk to 1 cup (let stand 5-10 minutes)

MILK
1 Cup
1 cup non-dairy milk; OR 1 cup water OR juice; OR 1/4 cup dry powdered milk + 1 cup water; OR 2/3 cup evaporated milk + 1/3 cup water

BEEF/CHICKEN BROTH
1 Cup
1 cup vegetable broth; OR 1 bouillon cub (1 tsp granules or soup base) + 1 cup hot water, OR 1 tbsp soy sauce + 3/4 cup + 3 tbsp water

BUTTER
1 Cup
7/8 cup vegetable oil + 1/2 tsp salt (omit salt for unsalted butter); OR coconut oil, unsweetened apple sauce

CAKE FLOUR
1 Cup
3/4 cup + 2 tbsp all-purpose flour + 2 tbsp cornstarch

MAYONNAISE
1 Cup
1 cup plain yogurt; OR 1 cup sour cream

SOUR CREAM
1 Cup
1 cup plain yogurt; OR 3/4 cup buttermilk + 1/3 cup butter; OR 1 tbsp lemon juice OR vinegar + 3/4 cup + 3 tbsp cream

FRESH HERBS
To equal 1 tbsp fresh herbs substitute 1 teaspoon dried. Dried herbs are generally more potent & concentrated than fresh herbs

CREAM OF TARTAR
1/2 Teaspoon
1/2 tsp white vinegar or lemon juice

EGG
1 Egg
1/4 cup vegetable oil; 1/4 cup mashed banana, 1/4 cup unsweetened applesauce OR 1 tbsp ground flaxseed with 3 tbsp water, stir to combine, and let stand for 5 minutes to thicken

BALSAMIC VINEGAR
1 Tbsp
1 tbsp cider vinegar or red wine vinegar + 1/2 tsp sugar

TOMATO SAUCE
2 Cups
3/4 cup tomato paste + 1 cup water; mix to combine

SOYA SAUCE
1/2 Cup
1/2 cup coconut aminos OR liquid aminos OR 1/4 cup worcestershire sauce + 1 tbsp water

Contents

	hors d'oeuvre	Appetizer	Soup	Salad	Main Course	Dessert	Other
Recipe N° 001 Sticky toffee pudding	○	○	○	○	○	✓	
Recipe N° 002 Kimchi	○	○	○	○	○	○	side
Recipe N° 003	○	○	○	○	○	○	
Recipe N° 004	○	○	○	○	○	○	
Recipe N° 005	○	○	○	○	○	○	
Recipe N° 006	○	○	○	○	○	○	
Recipe N° 007	○	○	○	○	○	○	
Recipe N° 008	○	○	○	○	○	○	
Recipe N° 009	○	○	○	○	○	○	
Recipe N° 010	○	○	○	○	○	○	
Recipe N° 011	○	○	○	○	○	○	
Recipe N° 012	○	○	○	○	○	○	
Recipe N° 013	○	○	○	○	○	○	
Recipe N° 014	○	○	○	○	○	○	
Recipe N° 015	○	○	○	○	○	○	
Recipe N° 016	○	○	○	○	○	○	
Recipe N° 017	○	○	○	○	○	○	
Recipe N° 018	○	○	○	○	○	○	
Recipe N° 019	○	○	○	○	○	○	
Recipe N° 020	○	○	○	○	○	○	
Recipe N° 021	○	○	○	○	○	○	
Recipe N° 022	○	○	○	○	○	○	
Recipe N° 023	○	○	○	○	○	○	
Recipe N° 024	○	○	○	○	○	○	
Recipe N° 025	○	○	○	○	○	○	
Recipe N° 026	○	○	○	○	○	○	
Recipe N° 027	○	○	○	○	○	○	
Recipe N° 028	○	○	○	○	○	○	
Recipe N° 029	○	○	○	○	○	○	
Recipe N° 030	○	○	○	○	○	○	

Contents

	hors d'oeuvre	Appetizer	Soup	Salad	Main Course	Dessert	Other
Recipe N° 031	○	○	○	○	○	○	
Recipe N° 032	○	○	○	○	○	○	
Recipe N° 033	○	○	○	○	○	○	
Recipe N° 034	○	○	○	○	○	○	
Recipe N° 035	○	○	○	○	○	○	
Recipe N° 036	○	○	○	○	○	○	
Recipe N° 037	○	○	○	○	○	○	
Recipe N° 038	○	○	○	○	○	○	
Recipe N° 039	○	○	○	○	○	○	
Recipe N° 040	○	○	○	○	○	○	
Recipe N° 041	○	○	○	○	○	○	
Recipe N° 042	○	○	○	○	○	○	
Recipe N° 043	○	○	○	○	○	○	
Recipe N° 044	○	○	○	○	○	○	
Recipe N° 045	○	○	○	○	○	○	
Recipe N° 046	○	○	○	○	○	○	
Recipe N° 047	○	○	○	○	○	○	
Recipe N° 048	○	○	○	○	○	○	
Recipe N° 049	○	○	○	○	○	○	
Recipe N° 050	○	○	○	○	○	○	
Recipe N° 051	○	○	○	○	○	○	
Recipe N° 052	○	○	○	○	○	○	
Recipe N° 053	○	○	○	○	○	○	
Recipe N° 054	○	○	○	○	○	○	
Recipe N° 055	○	○	○	○	○	○	
Recipe N° 056	○	○	○	○	○	○	
Recipe N° 057	○	○	○	○	○	○	
Recipe N° 058	○	○	○	○	○	○	
Recipe N° 059	○	○	○	○	○	○	
Recipe N° 060	○	○	○	○	○	○	

Contents

	hors d'oeuvre	Appetizer	Soup	Salad	Main Course	Dessert	Other
Recipe N° 061	○	○	○	○	○	○	
Recipe N° 062	○	○	○	○	○	○	
Recipe N° 063	○	○	○	○	○	○	
Recipe N° 064	○	○	○	○	○	○	
Recipe N° 065	○	○	○	○	○	○	
Recipe N° 066	○	○	○	○	○	○	
Recipe N° 067	○	○	○	○	○	○	
Recipe N° 068	○	○	○	○	○	○	
Recipe N° 069	○	○	○	○	○	○	
Recipe N° 070	○	○	○	○	○	○	
Recipe N° 071	○	○	○	○	○	○	
Recipe N° 072	○	○	○	○	○	○	
Recipe N° 073	○	○	○	○	○	○	
Recipe N° 074	○	○	○	○	○	○	
Recipe N° 075	○	○	○	○	○	○	
Recipe N° 076	○	○	○	○	○	○	
Recipe N° 077	○	○	○	○	○	○	
Recipe N° 078	○	○	○	○	○	○	
Recipe N° 079	○	○	○	○	○	○	
Recipe N° 080	○	○	○	○	○	○	
Recipe N° 081	○	○	○	○	○	○	
Recipe N° 082	○	○	○	○	○	○	
Recipe N° 083	○	○	○	○	○	○	
Recipe N° 084	○	○	○	○	○	○	
Recipe N° 085	○	○	○	○	○	○	
Recipe N° 086	○	○	○	○	○	○	
Recipe N° 087	○	○	○	○	○	○	
Recipe N° 088	○	○	○	○	○	○	
Recipe N° 089	○	○	○	○	○	○	
Recipe N° 090	○	○	○	○	○	○	

Contents

	hors d'oeuvre	Appetizer	Soup	Salad	Main Course	Dessert	Other
Recipe N° 091	○	○	○	○	○	○	
Recipe N° 092	○	○	○	○	○	○	
Recipe N° 093	○	○	○	○	○	○	
Recipe N° 094	○	○	○	○	○	○	
Recipe N° 095	○	○	○	○	○	○	
Recipe N° 096	○	○	○	○	○	○	
Recipe N° 097	○	○	○	○	○	○	
Recipe N° 098	○	○	○	○	○	○	
Recipe N° 099	○	○	○	○	○	○	
Recipe N° 100	○	○	○	○	○	○	
Recipe N° 101	○	○	○	○	○	○	
Recipe N° 102	○	○	○	○	○	○	
Recipe N° 103	○	○	○	○	○	○	
Recipe N° 104	○	○	○	○	○	○	
Recipe N° 105	○	○	○	○	○	○	
Recipe N° 106	○	○	○	○	○	○	
Recipe N° 107	○	○	○	○	○	○	
Recipe N° 108	○	○	○	○	○	○	
Recipe N° 109	○	○	○	○	○	○	
Recipe N° 110	○	○	○	○	○	○	
Recipe N° 111	○	○	○	○	○	○	
Recipe N° 112	○	○	○	○	○	○	
Recipe N° 113	○	○	○	○	○	○	
Recipe N° 114	○	○	○	○	○	○	
Recipe N° 115	○	○	○	○	○	○	
Recipe N° 116	○	○	○	○	○	○	
Recipe N° 117	○	○	○	○	○	○	
Recipe N° 118	○	○	○	○	○	○	
Recipe N° 119	○	○	○	○	○	○	
Recipe N° 120	○	○	○	○	○	○	

Contents

	hors d'oeuvre	Appetizer	Soup	Salad	Main Course	Dessert	Other
Recipe N° 121	○	○	○	○	○	○	
Recipe N° 122	○	○	○	○	○	○	
Recipe N° 123	○	○	○	○	○	○	
Recipe N° 124	○	○	○	○	○	○	
Recipe N° 125	○	○	○	○	○	○	
Recipe N° 126	○	○	○	○	○	○	
Recipe N° 127	○	○	○	○	○	○	
Recipe N° 128	○	○	○	○	○	○	
Recipe N° 129	○	○	○	○	○	○	
Recipe N° 130	○	○	○	○	○	○	
Recipe N° 131	○	○	○	○	○	○	
Recipe N° 132	○	○	○	○	○	○	
Recipe N° 133	○	○	○	○	○	○	
Recipe N° 134	○	○	○	○	○	○	
Recipe N° 135	○	○	○	○	○	○	
Recipe N° 136	○	○	○	○	○	○	
Recipe N° 137	○	○	○	○	○	○	
Recipe N° 138	○	○	○	○	○	○	
Recipe N° 139	○	○	○	○	○	○	
Recipe N° 140	○	○	○	○	○	○	
Recipe N° 141	○	○	○	○	○	○	
Recipe N° 142	○	○	○	○	○	○	
Recipe N° 143	○	○	○	○	○	○	
Recipe N° 144	○	○	○	○	○	○	
Recipe N° 145	○	○	○	○	○	○	
Recipe N° 146	○	○	○	○	○	○	
Recipe N° 147	○	○	○	○	○	○	
Recipe N° 148	○	○	○	○	○	○	
Recipe N° 149	○	○	○	○	○	○	
Recipe N° 150	○	○	○	○	○	○	

Recipe: Sticky toffee pudding

Prep Time: 10

Cook Time: 15 - 30 mins

Oven Temp: 190 c

Calories: 194 per 1 pud

Star Rating:

✓ ✓ ✓ ✓ ✓

Tried and tested!

\# Recipe nº: 1

Source: Thebigmansworld.com

Yeild: 6

Serves: 6? 1? ☺

Ingredients:

100g	dates	50g	golden syrup	) for sauce
125ml	milk	100g	brown sugar	
50ml	water	80g	butter	
0.5tsp	baking soda			
56g	butter			
55g	brown sugar			
100g	self raising flour.			

Directions:

① Add dates, milk and water into saucepan and simmer until dates are softened. Remove from heat and add baking soda, mix and let cool.

② In a mixing bowl mix sugar and butter until smooth, slowly add date mixture. Add flour until fully combined. Transfer to baking dish.

③ Bake for 20 mins (+ depending if making more).

Sauce

① Add all ingredients and simmer for 5 mins.

Serve cake with the sauce and ice cream or cream.

Notes:

Use ramekins or one big dish, however you prefer.

Recipe: Kimchi

Star Rating: ☆ ☆ ☆ ☆ ☆

Prep Time: _____

Cook Time: _____

Oven Temp: _____

Calories: _____

Recipe Nº: 2

Source: _____

Yeild: _____

Serves: _____

Ingredients:

_____ _____

_____ _____

_____ _____

_____ _____

_____ _____

_____ _____

Directions:

_____

_____

_____

_____

_____

_____

_____

_____

_____

_____

_____

_____

_____

_____

Notes:

_____

_____

_____

Recipe: _____

Star Rating: ☆ ☆ ☆ ☆ ☆

Prep Time: _____

Cook Time: _____

Oven Temp: _____

Calories: _____

Recipe N°: _____

Source: _____

Yeild: _____

Serves: _____

Ingredients.

_____ _____

_____ _____

_____ _____

_____ _____

_____ _____

_____ _____

Directions.

_____

_____

_____

_____

_____

_____

_____

_____

_____

_____

_____

_____

_____

Notes.

_____

_____

_____

Recipe: _____

Star Rating: ☆ ☆ ☆ ☆ ☆

Prep Time: _____

Cook Time: _____

Oven Temp: _____

Calories: _____

Recipe N°: _____

Source: _____

Yeild: _____

Serves: _____

Ingredients:

_____   _____

_____   _____

_____   _____

_____   _____

_____   _____

_____   _____

_____   _____

Directions:

_____

_____

_____

_____

_____

_____

_____

_____

_____

_____

_____

_____

_____

_____

Notes:

_____

_____

_____

Recipe: _____

Star Rating: ☆ ☆ ☆ ☆ ☆

Prep Time: _____

Cook Time: _____

Oven Temp: _____

Calories: _____

Recipe N°: _____

Source: _____

Yeild: _____

Serves: _____

Ingredients

_____ _____ _____

_____ _____ _____

_____ _____ _____

_____ _____ _____

_____ _____ _____

Directions

_____

_____

_____

_____

_____

_____

_____

_____

_____

_____

_____

_____

_____

_____

_____

_____

Notes

_____

_____

_____

Recipe: _____

Star Rating: ☆ ☆ ☆ ☆ ☆

Prep Time: _____

Cook Time: _____

Oven Temp: _____

Calories: _____

Recipe Nº: _____

Source: _____

Yeild: _____

Serves: _____

Ingredients:

_____ _____

_____ _____

_____ _____

_____ _____

_____ _____

_____ _____

Directions:

_____

_____

_____

_____

_____

_____

_____

_____

_____

_____

_____

_____

_____

_____

Notes:

_____

_____

_____

Recipe: _____

Star Rating: ☆ ☆ ☆ ☆ ☆

Prep Time: _____

Cook Time: _____

Oven Temp: _____

Calories: _____

Recipe N°: _____

Source: _____

Yeild: _____

Serves: _____

Ingredients:

_____   _____

_____   _____

_____   _____

_____   _____

_____   _____

_____   _____

Directions:

_____

_____

_____

_____

_____

_____

_____

_____

_____

_____

_____

_____

_____

Notes:

_____

_____

_____

Recipe: _____

Star Rating: ☆ ☆ ☆ ☆ ☆

Prep Time: _____

Cook Time: _____

Oven Temp: _____

Calories: _____

\# Recipe N°: _____

Source: _____

Yeild: _____

Serves: _____

Ingredients:

_____ _____

_____ _____

_____ _____

_____ _____

_____ _____

_____ _____

_____ _____

Directions:

_____

_____

_____

_____

_____

_____

_____

_____

_____

_____

_____

_____

_____

_____

_____

Notes:

_____

_____

_____

Recipe: _____

Star Rating: ☆ ☆ ☆ ☆ ☆

Prep Time: _____

Cook Time: _____

Oven Temp: _____

Calories: _____

Recipe Nº: _____

Source: _____

Yeild: _____

Serves: _____

Ingredients:

_____ _____ _____ _____

_____ _____ _____ _____

_____ _____ _____ _____

_____ _____ _____ _____

_____ _____ _____ _____

_____ _____ _____ _____

Directions:

_____

_____

_____

_____

_____

_____

_____

_____

_____

_____

_____

_____

_____

_____

Notes:

_____

_____

_____

Recipe: _____

Star Rating: ☆ ☆ ☆ ☆ ☆

Prep Time: _____

Cook Time: _____

Oven Temp: _____

Calories: _____

\# Recipe Nº: _____

Source: _____

Yeild: _____

Serves: _____

Ingredients:

_____   _____

_____   _____

_____   _____

_____   _____

_____   _____

_____   _____

Directions:

_____

_____

_____

_____

_____

_____

_____

_____

_____

_____

_____

_____

_____

_____

Notes:

_____

_____

_____

Recipe: _____

Star Rating: ☆ ☆ ☆ ☆ ☆

Prep Time: _____

Cook Time: _____

Oven Temp: _____

Calories: _____

Recipe Nº: _____

Source: _____

Yeild: _____

Serves: _____

Ingredients

_____ _____ _____ _____

_____ _____ _____ _____

_____ _____ _____ _____

_____ _____ _____ _____

_____ _____ _____ _____

Directions

_____

_____

_____

_____

_____

_____

_____

_____

_____

_____

_____

_____

_____

Notes

_____

_____

_____

_____

Recipe: _____

Star Rating: ☆ ☆ ☆ ☆ ☆

Prep Time: _____

Cook Time: _____

Oven Temp: _____

Calories: _____

Recipe N°: _____

Source: _____

Yeild: _____

Serves: _____

Ingredients:

_____ _____

_____ _____

_____ _____

_____ _____

_____ _____

_____ _____

_____ _____

Directions:

_____

_____

_____

_____

_____

_____

_____

_____

_____

_____

_____

_____

_____

_____

_____

Notes:

_____

_____

_____

Recipe: _____

Star Rating: ☆ ☆ ☆ ☆ ☆

Prep Time: _____

Cook Time: _____

Oven Temp: _____

Calories: _____

Recipe N°: _____

Source: _____

Yeild: _____

Serves: _____

Ingredients:

_____   _____

_____   _____

_____   _____

_____   _____

_____   _____

Directions:

_____

_____

_____

_____

_____

_____

_____

_____

_____

_____

_____

Notes:

_____

_____

_____

Recipe: _____

Star Rating: ☆ ☆ ☆ ☆ ☆

Prep Time: _____

Cook Time: _____

Oven Temp: _____

Calories: _____

Recipe Nº: _____

Source: _____

Yeild: _____

Serves: _____

Ingredients:

_____ _____

_____ _____

_____ _____

_____ _____

_____ _____

_____ _____

_____ _____

Directions:

_____

_____

_____

_____

_____

_____

_____

_____

_____

_____

_____

_____

_____

Notes:

_____

_____

_____

Recipe: _____   Star Rating: ☆ ☆ ☆ ☆ ☆

Prep Time: _____

Cook Time: _____

Oven Temp: _____

Calories: _____

\# Recipe N°: _____

Source: _____

Yeild: _____

Serves: _____

Ingredients

_____   _____
_____   _____
_____   _____
_____   _____
_____   _____
_____   _____

Directions

_____
_____
_____
_____
_____
_____
_____
_____
_____
_____
_____
_____

Notes

_____
_____
_____

Recipe: _____

Star Rating: ☆ ☆ ☆ ☆ ☆

Prep Time: _____

Cook Time: _____

Oven Temp: _____

Calories: _____

Recipe N°: _____

Source: _____

Yeild: _____

Serves: _____

Ingredients:

_____ _____

_____ _____

_____ _____

_____ _____

_____ _____

_____ _____

_____ _____

Directions:

_____

_____

_____

_____

_____

_____

_____

_____

_____

_____

_____

_____

_____

_____

_____

Notes:

_____

_____

_____

Recipe: _____

Star Rating: ☆ ☆ ☆ ☆ ☆

Prep Time: _____

Cook Time: _____

Oven Temp: _____

Calories: _____

Recipe N°: _____

Source: _____

Yeild: _____

Serves: _____

Ingredients:

_____ _____

_____ _____

_____ _____

_____ _____

_____ _____

_____ _____

Directions:

_____

_____

_____

_____

_____

_____

_____

_____

_____

_____

_____

_____

_____

Notes:

_____

_____

_____

Recipe: _____

Star Rating: ☆ ☆ ☆ ☆ ☆

Prep Time: _____

Cook Time: _____

Oven Temp: _____

Calories: _____

Recipe N°: _____

Source: _____

Yeild: _____

Serves: _____

Ingredients

_____ _____

_____ _____

_____ _____

_____ _____

_____ _____

_____ _____

Directions

_____

_____

_____

_____

_____

_____

_____

_____

_____

_____

_____

_____

_____

_____

Notes

_____

_____

_____

Recipe: _____

Star Rating: ☆ ☆ ☆ ☆ ☆

Prep Time: _____

Cook Time: _____

Oven Temp: _____

Calories: _____

Recipe N°: _____

Source: _____

Yeild: _____

Serves: _____

Ingredients

_____ _____

_____ _____

_____ _____

_____ _____

_____ _____

Directions

_____

_____

_____

_____

_____

_____

_____

_____

_____

_____

_____

_____

_____

_____

_____

Notes

_____

_____

_____

Recipe: _____

Star Rating: ☆ ☆ ☆ ☆ ☆

Prep Time: _____

Cook Time: _____

Oven Temp: _____

Calories: _____

Recipe N°: _____

Source: _____

Yeild: _____

Serves: _____

Ingredients:

_____ _____ _____ _____
_____ _____ _____ _____
_____ _____ _____ _____
_____ _____ _____ _____
_____ _____ _____ _____
_____ _____ _____ _____
_____ _____ _____ _____

Directions:

_____
_____
_____
_____
_____
_____
_____
_____
_____
_____
_____
_____
_____
_____
_____

Notes:

_____
_____
_____

Recipe: _____

Star Rating: ☆ ☆ ☆ ☆ ☆

Prep Time: _____

Cook Time: _____

Oven Temp: _____

Calories: _____

Recipe N°: _____

Source: _____

Yeild: _____

Serves: _____

Ingredients:

_____ _____

_____ _____

_____ _____

_____ _____

_____ _____

_____ _____

Directions:

_____

_____

_____

_____

_____

_____

_____

_____

_____

_____

_____

_____

_____

_____

Notes:

_____

_____

_____

Recipe: _____

Star Rating: ☆ ☆ ☆ ☆ ☆

🔪🕐 Prep Time: _____

🍲🕐 Cook Time: _____

🔲📏 Oven Temp: _____

🧮🍎 Calories: _____

\# Recipe N°: _____

ⓘ Source: _____

🥤 Yeild: _____

🍽 Serves: _____

🥛 Ingredients:

_____ _____

_____ _____

_____ _____

_____ _____

_____ _____

_____ _____

_____ _____

🥄 Directions:

_____

_____

_____

_____

_____

_____

_____

_____

_____

_____

_____

_____

_____

_____

_____

📝 Notes:

_____

_____

_____

Recipe: _____

Star Rating: ☆ ☆ ☆ ☆ ☆

Prep Time: _____

Cook Time: _____

Oven Temp: _____

Calories: _____

\# Recipe N°: _____

Source: _____

Yeild: _____

Serves: _____

Ingredients

_____ _____

_____ _____

_____ _____

_____ _____

_____ _____

_____ _____

Directions

_____

_____

_____

_____

_____

_____

_____

_____

_____

_____

_____

_____

Notes

_____

_____

_____

Recipe: _____

Star Rating: ☆ ☆ ☆ ☆ ☆

Prep Time: _____
Cook Time: _____
Oven Temp: _____
Calories: _____

Recipe N°: _____
Source: _____
Yeild: _____
Serves: _____

Ingredients:

_____ _____
_____ _____
_____ _____
_____ _____
_____ _____
_____ _____
_____ _____

Directions:

_____
_____
_____
_____
_____
_____
_____
_____
_____
_____
_____
_____
_____
_____
_____

Notes:

_____
_____
_____

Recipe: _____

Star Rating: ☆ ☆ ☆ ☆ ☆

Prep Time: _____

Cook Time: _____

Oven Temp: _____

Calories: _____

Recipe N°: _____

Source: _____

Yeild: _____

Serves: _____

Ingredients.

_____ _____
_____ _____
_____ _____
_____ _____
_____ _____
_____ _____

Directions.

_____
_____
_____
_____
_____
_____
_____
_____
_____
_____
_____
_____

Notes.

_____
_____
_____

Recipe: _____

Star Rating: ☆ ☆ ☆ ☆ ☆

Prep Time: _____

Cook Time: _____

Oven Temp: _____

Calories: _____

Recipe Nº: _____

Source: _____

Yeild: _____

Serves: _____

Ingredients:

_____   _____
_____   _____
_____   _____
_____   _____
_____   _____
_____   _____

Directions:

_____
_____
_____
_____
_____
_____
_____
_____
_____
_____
_____
_____
_____
_____

Notes:

_____
_____
_____

Recipe: _____

Star Rating: ☆ ☆ ☆ ☆ ☆

Prep Time: _____

Cook Time: _____

Oven Temp: _____

Calories: _____

Recipe N°: _____

Source: _____

Yeild: _____

Serves: _____

Ingredients

_____   _____

_____   _____

_____   _____

_____   _____

_____   _____

_____   _____

_____   _____

Directions

_____

_____

_____

_____

_____

_____

_____

_____

_____

_____

_____

_____

_____

Notes

_____

_____

_____

Recipe:

Star Rating: ☆ ☆ ☆ ☆ ☆

Prep Time: _____

Cook Time: _____

Oven Temp: _____

Calories: _____

Recipe Nº: _____

Source: _____

Yeild: _____

Serves: _____

Ingredients:

_____ _____

_____ _____

_____ _____

_____ _____

_____ _____

_____ _____

Directions:

_____

_____

_____

_____

_____

_____

_____

_____

_____

_____

_____

_____

_____

_____

_____

_____

Notes:

_____

_____

_____

Recipe: _____

Star Rating: ☆ ☆ ☆ ☆ ☆

Prep Time: _____

Cook Time: _____

Oven Temp: _____

Calories: _____

Recipe N°: _____

Source: _____

Yeild: _____

Serves: _____

Ingredients.

_____ _____
_____ _____
_____ _____
_____ _____
_____ _____
_____ _____

Directions.

_____
_____
_____
_____
_____
_____
_____
_____
_____
_____
_____
_____

Notes.

_____
_____
_____

Recipe: _____

Star Rating: ☆ ☆ ☆ ☆ ☆

Prep Time: _____

Cook Time: _____

Oven Temp: _____

Calories: _____

Recipe N°: _____

Source: _____

Yeild: _____

Serves: _____

Ingredients:

_____ _____

_____ _____

_____ _____

_____ _____

_____ _____

_____ _____

_____ _____

Directions:

_____

_____

_____

_____

_____

_____

_____

_____

_____

_____

_____

_____

_____

_____

Notes:

_____

_____

_____

Recipe: _____

Star Rating: ☆ ☆ ☆ ☆ ☆

Prep Time: _____

Cook Time: _____

Oven Temp: _____

Calories: _____

Recipe N°: _____

Source: _____

Yeild: _____

Serves: _____

Ingredients.

_____ _____

_____ _____

_____ _____

_____ _____

_____ _____

_____ _____

Directions.

_____

_____

_____

_____

_____

_____

_____

_____

_____

_____

_____

_____

_____

_____

Notes.

_____

_____

_____

Recipe: _____

Star Rating: ☆ ☆ ☆ ☆ ☆

Prep Time: _____

Cook Time: _____

Oven Temp: _____

Calories: _____

Recipe N°: _____

Source: _____

Yeild: _____

Serves: _____

Ingredients:

_____ _____

_____ _____

_____ _____

_____ _____

_____ _____

_____ _____

_____ _____

Directions:

_____

_____

_____

_____

_____

_____

_____

_____

_____

_____

_____

_____

_____

_____

_____

_____

_____

Notes:

_____

_____

_____

Recipe:

Star Rating: ☆ ☆ ☆ ☆ ☆

Prep Time:

Cook Time:

Oven Temp:

Calories:

\# Recipe Nº:

Source:

Yeild:

Serves:

Ingredients:

Directions:

Notes:

Recipe: _____

Star Rating: ☆ ☆ ☆ ☆ ☆

Prep Time: _____

Cook Time: _____

Oven Temp: _____

Calories: _____

Recipe N°: _____

Source: _____

Yeild: _____

Serves: _____

Ingredients:

_____ _____

_____ _____

_____ _____

_____ _____

_____ _____

_____ _____

Directions:

_____

_____

_____

_____

_____

_____

_____

_____

_____

_____

_____

_____

_____

_____

Notes:

_____

_____

_____

Recipe: _____

Star Rating: ☆ ☆ ☆ ☆ ☆

Prep Time: _____

Cook Time: _____

Oven Temp: _____

Calories: _____

Recipe N°: _____

Source: _____

Yeild: _____

Serves: _____

Ingredients:

_____ _____

_____ _____

_____ _____

_____ _____

_____ _____

_____ _____

Directions:

_____

_____

_____

_____

_____

_____

_____

_____

_____

_____

Notes:

_____

_____

Recipe: _____

Star Rating: ☆ ☆ ☆ ☆ ☆

Prep Time: _____

Cook Time: _____

Oven Temp: _____

Calories: _____

Recipe N°: _____

Source: _____

Yeild: _____

Serves: _____

Ingredients:

_____   _____   _____   _____

_____   _____   _____   _____

_____   _____   _____   _____

_____   _____   _____   _____

_____   _____   _____   _____

_____   _____   _____   _____

Directions:

_____

_____

_____

_____

_____

_____

_____

_____

_____

_____

_____

_____

_____

_____

_____

Notes:

_____

_____

_____

Recipe: _____

Star Rating: ☆ ☆ ☆ ☆ ☆

Prep Time: _____

Cook Time: _____

Oven Temp: _____

Calories: _____

Recipe N°: _____

Source: _____

Yeild: _____

Serves: _____

Ingredients:

_____ _____

_____ _____

_____ _____

_____ _____

_____ _____

_____ _____

Directions:

_____

_____

_____

_____

_____

_____

_____

_____

_____

_____

_____

_____

_____

Notes:

_____

_____

_____

Recipe: _____

Star Rating: ☆ ☆ ☆ ☆ ☆

Prep Time: _____

Cook Time: _____

Oven Temp: _____

Calories: _____

Recipe N°: _____

Source: _____

Yeild: _____

Serves: _____

Ingredients:

_____   _____

_____   _____

_____   _____

_____   _____

_____   _____

_____   _____

_____   _____

Directions:

_____

_____

_____

_____

_____

_____

_____

_____

_____

_____

_____

_____

_____

Notes:

_____

_____

_____

Recipe:

Star Rating: ☆ ☆ ☆ ☆ ☆

- Prep Time:
- Cook Time:
- Oven Temp:
- Calories:

- # Recipe N°:
- Source:
- Yeild:
- Serves:

Ingredients.

Directions.

Notes.

Recipe: _____

Star Rating: ☆ ☆ ☆ ☆ ☆

Prep Time: _____

Cook Time: _____

Oven Temp: _____

Calories: _____

Recipe N°: _____

Source: _____

Yeild: _____

Serves: _____

Ingredients:

_____ _____

_____ _____

_____ _____

_____ _____

_____ _____

_____ _____

_____ _____

Directions:

_____

_____

_____

_____

_____

_____

_____

_____

_____

_____

_____

_____

_____

_____

_____

Notes:

_____

_____

_____

Recipe: _____

Star Rating: ☆ ☆ ☆ ☆ ☆

Prep Time: _____

Cook Time: _____

Oven Temp: _____

Calories: _____

Recipe N°: _____

Source: _____

Yeild: _____

Serves: _____

Ingredients

_____ _____
_____ _____
_____ _____
_____ _____
_____ _____
_____ _____

Directions

_____
_____
_____
_____
_____
_____
_____
_____
_____
_____
_____
_____
_____

Notes

_____
_____
_____

Recipe: _____

Star Rating: ☆ ☆ ☆ ☆ ☆

Prep Time: _____

Cook Time: _____

Oven Temp: _____

Calories: _____

Recipe N°: _____

Source: _____

Yeild: _____

Serves: _____

Ingredients:

_____ _____
_____ _____
_____ _____
_____ _____
_____ _____
_____ _____

Directions:

_____
_____
_____
_____
_____
_____
_____
_____
_____
_____
_____
_____
_____
_____

Notes:

_____
_____
_____

Recipe: _____

Star Rating: ☆ ☆ ☆ ☆ ☆

Prep Time: _____

Cook Time: _____

Oven Temp: _____

Calories: _____

Recipe Nº: _____

Source: _____

Yeild: _____

Serves: _____

Ingredients:

_____ _____

_____ _____

_____ _____

_____ _____

_____ _____

Directions:

_____

_____

_____

_____

_____

_____

_____

_____

_____

_____

Notes:

_____

_____

_____

Recipe: _____

Star Rating: ☆ ☆ ☆ ☆ ☆

Prep Time: _____
Cook Time: _____
Oven Temp: _____
Calories: _____

Recipe N°: _____
Source: _____
Yeild: _____
Serves: _____

Ingredients:

_____   _____
_____   _____
_____   _____
_____   _____
_____   _____
_____   _____

Directions:

_____
_____
_____
_____
_____
_____
_____
_____
_____
_____
_____
_____
_____
_____

Notes:

_____
_____
_____

Recipe: _____   Star Rating: ☆ ☆ ☆ ☆ ☆

Prep Time: _____

Cook Time: _____

Oven Temp: _____

Calories: _____

Recipe N°: _____

Source: _____

Yeild: _____

Serves: _____

Ingredients

_____   _____

_____   _____

_____   _____

_____   _____

_____   _____

_____   _____

Directions

_____

_____

_____

_____

_____

_____

_____

_____

_____

_____

_____

_____

Notes

_____

_____

_____

Recipe: _____

Star Rating: ☆ ☆ ☆ ☆ ☆

Prep Time: _____

Cook Time: _____

Oven Temp: _____

Calories: _____

Recipe N°: _____

Source: _____

Yeild: _____

Serves: _____

Ingredients:

_____ _____

_____ _____

_____ _____

_____ _____

_____ _____

_____ _____

_____ _____

Directions:

_____

_____

_____

_____

_____

_____

_____

_____

_____

_____

_____

_____

_____

_____

_____

Notes:

_____

_____

_____

Recipe: _____

Star Rating: ☆ ☆ ☆ ☆ ☆

Prep Time: _____

Cook Time: _____

Oven Temp: _____

Calories: _____

\# Recipe N°: _____

Source: _____

Yeild: _____

Serves: _____

Ingredients:

_____ _____ _____ _____

_____ _____ _____ _____

_____ _____ _____ _____

_____ _____ _____ _____

_____ _____ _____ _____

_____ _____ _____ _____

Directions:

_____

_____

_____

_____

_____

_____

_____

_____

_____

_____

_____

_____

Notes:

_____

_____

_____

Recipe: _____

Star Rating: ☆ ☆ ☆ ☆ ☆

Prep Time: _____

Cook Time: _____

Oven Temp: _____

Calories: _____

Recipe N°: _____

Source: _____

Yeild: _____

Serves: _____

Ingredients:

_____   _____

_____   _____

_____   _____

_____   _____

_____   _____

_____   _____

_____   _____

Directions:

_____

_____

_____

_____

_____

_____

_____

_____

_____

_____

_____

_____

_____

_____

_____

Notes:

_____

_____

_____

Recipe: _____

Star Rating: ☆ ☆ ☆ ☆ ☆

- Prep Time: _____
- Cook Time: _____
- Oven Temp: _____
- Calories: _____

- # Recipe N°: _____
- Source: _____
- Yeild: _____
- Serves: _____

Ingredients:

_____ _____
_____ _____
_____ _____
_____ _____
_____ _____
_____ _____

Directions:

_____
_____
_____
_____
_____
_____
_____
_____
_____
_____
_____

Notes:

_____
_____
_____

Recipe: _____

Star Rating: ☆ ☆ ☆ ☆ ☆

Prep Time: _____

Cook Time: _____

Oven Temp: _____

Calories: _____

Recipe N°: _____

Source: _____

Yeild: _____

Serves: _____

Ingredients:

_____ _____

_____ _____

_____ _____

_____ _____

_____ _____

_____ _____

_____ _____

Directions:

_____

_____

_____

_____

_____

_____

_____

_____

_____

_____

_____

_____

_____

_____

Notes.

_____

_____

_____

Recipe: _____

Star Rating: ☆ ☆ ☆ ☆ ☆

Prep Time: _____

Cook Time: _____

Oven Temp: _____

Calories: _____

Recipe N°: _____

Source: _____

Yeild: _____

Serves: _____

Ingredients:

_____ _____

_____ _____

_____ _____

_____ _____

_____ _____

_____ _____

Directions:

_____

_____

_____

_____

_____

_____

_____

_____

_____

_____

_____

_____

Notes:

_____

_____

_____

Recipe: _____

Star Rating: ☆ ☆ ☆ ☆ ☆

Prep Time: _____

Cook Time: _____

Oven Temp: _____

Calories: _____

Recipe N°: _____

Source: _____

Yeild: _____

Serves: _____

Ingredients:

_____   _____

_____   _____

_____   _____

_____   _____

_____   _____

_____   _____

Directions:

_____

_____

_____

_____

_____

_____

_____

_____

_____

_____

_____

_____

_____

_____

_____

Notes:

_____

_____

_____

Recipe: _____

Star Rating: ☆ ☆ ☆ ☆ ☆

🔪🕐 Prep Time: _____

🍲🕐 Cook Time: _____

🔲🍴 Oven Temp: _____

🧮🍎 Calories: _____

\# Recipe N°: _____

ⓘ Source: _____

🥛 Yeild: _____

🍽 Serves: _____

🥛 Ingredients:

_____ _____
_____ _____
_____ _____
_____ _____
_____ _____
_____ _____

🍳 Directions:

_____
_____
_____
_____
_____
_____
_____
_____
_____
_____
_____
_____
_____

📝 Notes:

_____
_____
_____

Recipe: _____

Star Rating: ☆ ☆ ☆ ☆ ☆

Prep Time: _____

Cook Time: _____

Oven Temp: _____

Calories: _____

Recipe Nº: _____

Source: _____

Yeild: _____

Serves: _____

Ingredients:

_____ _____

_____ _____

_____ _____

_____ _____

_____ _____

_____ _____

_____ _____

Directions:

_____

_____

_____

_____

_____

_____

_____

_____

_____

_____

_____

_____

_____

_____

_____

Notes:

_____

_____

_____

Recipe: _____

Star Rating: ☆ ☆ ☆ ☆ ☆

Prep Time: _____

Cook Time: _____

Oven Temp: _____

Calories: _____

Recipe N°: _____

Source: _____

Yeild: _____

Serves: _____

Ingredients:

_____ _____

_____ _____

_____ _____

_____ _____

_____ _____

_____ _____

Directions:

_____

_____

_____

_____

_____

_____

_____

_____

_____

_____

_____

_____

_____

_____

_____

_____

Notes:

_____

_____

_____

_____

Recipe: _____

Star Rating: ☆ ☆ ☆ ☆ ☆

Prep Time: _____

Cook Time: _____

Oven Temp: _____

Calories: _____

Recipe N°: _____

Source: _____

Yeild: _____

Serves: _____

Ingredients:

_____ _____

_____ _____

_____ _____

_____ _____

_____ _____

_____ _____

_____ _____

Directions:

_____

_____

_____

_____

_____

_____

_____

_____

_____

_____

_____

_____

_____

_____

Notes:

_____

_____

_____

Recipe: _____

Star Rating: ☆ ☆ ☆ ☆ ☆

- Prep Time: _____
- Cook Time: _____
- Oven Temp: _____
- Calories: _____

- Recipe N°: _____
- Source: _____
- Yeild: _____
- Serves: _____

Ingredients:

_____ _____
_____ _____
_____ _____
_____ _____
_____ _____
_____ _____

Directions:

_____
_____
_____
_____
_____
_____
_____
_____
_____
_____
_____
_____
_____

Notes:

_____
_____
_____

Recipe: _____

Star Rating: ☆ ☆ ☆ ☆ ☆

Prep Time: _____

Cook Time: _____

Oven Temp: _____

Calories: _____

Recipe Nº: _____

Source: _____

Yeild: _____

Serves: _____

Ingredients.

_____ _____

_____ _____

_____ _____

_____ _____

_____ _____

_____ _____

Directions.

_____

_____

_____

_____

_____

_____

_____

_____

_____

_____

_____

_____

_____

_____

Notes.

_____

_____

_____

Recipe: _____

Star Rating: ☆ ☆ ☆ ☆ ☆

Prep Time: _____

Cook Time: _____

Oven Temp: _____

Calories: _____

Recipe Nº: _____

Source: _____

Yeild: _____

Serves: _____

Ingredients:

_____ _____
_____ _____
_____ _____
_____ _____
_____ _____
_____ _____

Directions:

_____
_____
_____
_____
_____
_____
_____
_____
_____
_____
_____
_____

Notes:

_____
_____
_____

Recipe: _____

Star Rating: ☆ ☆ ☆ ☆ ☆

Prep Time: _____

Cook Time: _____

Oven Temp: _____

Calories: _____

Recipe N°: _____

Source: _____

Yeild: _____

Serves: _____

Ingredients.

_____ _____

_____ _____

_____ _____

_____ _____

_____ _____

_____ _____

_____ _____

Directions.

_____

_____

_____

_____

_____

_____

_____

_____

_____

_____

_____

_____

_____

_____

Notes.

_____

_____

_____

Recipe: _____

Star Rating: ☆ ☆ ☆ ☆ ☆

Prep Time: _____

Cook Time: _____

Oven Temp: _____

Calories: _____

Recipe N°: _____

Source: _____

Yeild: _____

Serves: _____

Ingredients:

_____ _____

_____ _____

_____ _____

_____ _____

_____ _____

_____ _____

Directions:

_____

_____

_____

_____

_____

_____

_____

_____

_____

_____

_____

_____

Notes:

_____

_____

_____

Recipe: _____

Star Rating: ☆ ☆ ☆ ☆ ☆

🔪🕐 Prep Time: _____

🍲🕐 Cook Time: _____

⬛ Oven Temp: _____

🧮🍎 Calories: _____

\# Recipe Nº: _____

ⓘ Source: _____

🥛 Yeild: _____

🍽 Serves: _____

Ingredients

_____ _____ _____ _____

_____ _____ _____ _____

_____ _____ _____ _____

_____ _____ _____ _____

_____ _____ _____ _____

_____ _____ _____ _____

Directions

_____

_____

_____

_____

_____

_____

_____

_____

_____

_____

_____

_____

_____

_____

Notes

_____

_____

_____

Recipe: _____

Star Rating: ☆ ☆ ☆ ☆ ☆

Prep Time: _____

Cook Time: _____

Oven Temp: _____

Calories: _____

Recipe N°: _____

Source: _____

Yeild: _____

Serves: _____

Ingredients:

_____ _____

_____ _____

_____ _____

_____ _____

_____ _____

_____ _____

Directions:

_____

_____

_____

_____

_____

_____

_____

_____

_____

_____

_____

_____

Notes:

_____

_____

_____

Recipe: _____

Star Rating: ☆ ☆ ☆ ☆ ☆

⌖ 🕐 Prep Time: _____

🍲 🕐 Cook Time: _____

▭ 🥄 Oven Temp: _____

🔢 🍎 Calories: _____

Recipe N°: _____

Source: _____

Yeild: _____

Serves: _____

Ingredients:

_____ _____
_____ _____
_____ _____
_____ _____
_____ _____
_____ _____

Directions:

_____
_____
_____
_____
_____
_____
_____
_____
_____
_____
_____
_____
_____
_____
_____
_____
_____

Notes:

_____
_____
_____

Recipe: _____

Star Rating: ☆ ☆ ☆ ☆ ☆

🖊️🕐 Prep Time: _____

🍲🕐 Cook Time: _____

🔲📍 Oven Temp: _____

🔢🍎 Calories: _____

\# Recipe N°: _____

ℹ️ Source: _____

🥛 Yeild: _____

🍽️ Serves: _____

🥚 Ingredients:

_____ _____

_____ _____

_____ _____

_____ _____

_____ _____

_____ _____

🥄 Directions:

_____

_____

_____

_____

_____

_____

_____

_____

_____

_____

_____

_____

📝 Notes:

_____

_____

_____

_____

Recipe: _____

Star Rating: ☆ ☆ ☆ ☆ ☆

Prep Time: _____

Cook Time: _____

Oven Temp: _____

Calories: _____

Recipe N°: _____

Source: _____

Yeild: _____

Serves: _____

Ingredients:

_____ _____ _____ _____

_____ _____ _____ _____

_____ _____ _____ _____

_____ _____ _____ _____

_____ _____ _____ _____

_____ _____ _____ _____

_____ _____ _____ _____

Directions:

_____

_____

_____

_____

_____

_____

_____

_____

_____

_____

_____

_____

_____

_____

Notes:

_____

_____

_____

Recipe: _____   Star Rating: ☆ ☆ ☆ ☆ ☆

Prep Time: _____   # Recipe N°: _____
Cook Time: _____   Source: _____
Oven Temp: _____   Yeild: _____
Calories: _____   Serves: _____

Ingredients:

_____ _____
_____ _____
_____ _____
_____ _____
_____ _____
_____ _____

Directions:

_____
_____
_____
_____
_____
_____
_____
_____
_____
_____
_____

Notes:

_____
_____
_____

Recipe: _____

Star Rating: ☆ ☆ ☆ ☆ ☆

Prep Time: _____

Cook Time: _____

Oven Temp: _____

Calories: _____

Recipe N°: _____

Source: _____

Yeild: _____

Serves: _____

Ingredients:

_____ _____

_____ _____

_____ _____

_____ _____

_____ _____

_____ _____

_____ _____

Directions:

_____

_____

_____

_____

_____

_____

_____

_____

_____

_____

_____

_____

_____

_____

_____

Notes:

_____

_____

_____

Recipe:

Star Rating: ☆ ☆ ☆ ☆ ☆

Prep Time:

Cook Time:

Oven Temp:

Calories:

Recipe N°:

Source:

Yeild:

Serves:

Ingredients:

_____ _____
_____ _____
_____ _____
_____ _____
_____ _____
_____ _____

Directions:

_____
_____
_____
_____
_____
_____
_____
_____
_____
_____
_____
_____
_____
_____
_____

Notes:

_____
_____
_____

Recipe: _____

Star Rating: ☆ ☆ ☆ ☆ ☆

- Prep Time: _____
- Cook Time: _____
- Oven Temp: _____
- Calories: _____

- # Recipe Nº: _____
- Source: _____
- Yeild: _____
- Serves: _____

Ingredients:

_____ _____
_____ _____
_____ _____
_____ _____
_____ _____
_____ _____
_____ _____

Directions:

_____
_____
_____
_____
_____
_____
_____
_____
_____
_____
_____
_____
_____
_____
_____
_____

Notes:

_____
_____
_____

Recipe: _____

Star Rating: ☆ ☆ ☆ ☆ ☆

Prep Time: _____
Cook Time: _____
Oven Temp: _____
Calories: _____

Recipe n°: _____
Source: _____
Yeild: _____
Serves: _____

Ingredients:

_____ _____ _____ _____
_____ _____ _____ _____
_____ _____ _____ _____
_____ _____ _____ _____
_____ _____ _____ _____

Directions:

_____
_____
_____
_____
_____
_____
_____
_____
_____
_____
_____
_____

Notes:

_____
_____
_____

Recipe: _____

Star Rating: ☆ ☆ ☆ ☆ ☆

🔪⏱ Prep Time: _____

🍲⏱ Cook Time: _____

🔥🌡 Oven Temp: _____

🍎 Calories: _____

\# Recipe N°: _____

ⓘ Source: _____

🥤 Yeild: _____

🍽 Serves: _____

🥛 Ingredients:

_____ _____
_____ _____
_____ _____
_____ _____
_____ _____
_____ _____
_____ _____

🖌 Directions:

_____
_____
_____
_____
_____
_____
_____
_____
_____
_____
_____
_____
_____
_____
_____
_____
_____
_____

📝 Notes:

_____
_____
_____
_____

Recipe: _____

Star Rating: ☆ ☆ ☆ ☆ ☆

Prep Time: _____

Cook Time: _____

Oven Temp: _____

Calories: _____

Recipe N°: _____

Source: _____

Yeild: _____

Serves: _____

Ingredients.

_____ _____
_____ _____
_____ _____
_____ _____
_____ _____
_____ _____

Directions.

_____
_____
_____
_____
_____
_____
_____
_____
_____
_____
_____
_____
_____

Notes.

_____
_____
_____

Recipe: _____

Star Rating: ☆ ☆ ☆ ☆ ☆

Prep Time: _____

Cook Time: _____

Oven Temp: _____

Calories: _____

Recipe N°: _____

Source: _____

Yeild: _____

Serves: _____

Ingredients.

_____ _____
_____ _____
_____ _____
_____ _____
_____ _____
_____ _____

Directions.

_____
_____
_____
_____
_____
_____
_____
_____
_____
_____
_____
_____
_____
_____

Notes.

_____
_____
_____

Recipe: _____

Star Rating: ☆ ☆ ☆ ☆ ☆

Prep Time: _____

Cook Time: _____

Oven Temp: _____

Calories: _____

Recipe Nº: _____

Source: _____

Yeild: _____

Serves: _____

Ingredients:

_____   _____
_____   _____
_____   _____
_____   _____
_____   _____
_____   _____

Directions:

_____
_____
_____
_____
_____
_____
_____
_____
_____
_____
_____
_____
_____

Notes:

_____
_____
_____
_____

Recipe: _____

Star Rating: ☆ ☆ ☆ ☆ ☆

Prep Time: _____

Cook Time: _____

Oven Temp: _____

Calories: _____

Recipe N°: _____

Source: _____

Yeild: _____

Serves: _____

Ingredients:

_____ _____ _____ _____

_____ _____ _____ _____

_____ _____ _____ _____

_____ _____ _____ _____

_____ _____ _____ _____

_____ _____ _____ _____

Directions:

_____

_____

_____

_____

_____

_____

_____

_____

_____

_____

_____

_____

_____

Notes:

_____

_____

_____

Recipe: _____

Star Rating: ☆ ☆ ☆ ☆ ☆

Prep Time: _____

Cook Time: _____

Oven Temp: _____

Calories: _____

Recipe N°: _____

Source: _____

Yeild: _____

Serves: _____

Ingredients:

_____   _____
_____   _____
_____   _____
_____   _____
_____   _____
_____   _____

Directions:

_____
_____
_____
_____
_____
_____
_____
_____
_____
_____
_____
_____
_____

Notes:

_____
_____
_____

Recipe: _____

Star Rating: ☆ ☆ ☆ ☆ ☆

Prep Time: _____

Cook Time: _____

Oven Temp: _____

Calories: _____

Recipe N°: _____

Source: _____

Yeild: _____

Serves: _____

Ingredients:

_____ _____

_____ _____

_____ _____

_____ _____

_____ _____

_____ _____

Directions:

_____

_____

_____

_____

_____

_____

_____

_____

_____

_____

_____

_____

_____

_____

_____

Notes:

_____

_____

_____

Recipe: _____

Star Rating: ☆ ☆ ☆ ☆ ☆

Prep Time: _____

Cook Time: _____

Oven Temp: _____

Calories: _____

Recipe N°: _____

Source: _____

Yeild: _____

Serves: _____

Ingredients:

_____ _____

_____ _____

_____ _____

_____ _____

_____ _____

_____ _____

Directions:

_____

_____

_____

_____

_____

_____

_____

_____

_____

_____

_____

_____

Notes:

_____

_____

_____

Recipe: _____

Star Rating: ☆ ☆ ☆ ☆ ☆

Prep Time: _____

Cook Time: _____

Oven Temp: _____

Calories: _____

Recipe N°: _____

Source: _____

Yeild: _____

Serves: _____

Ingredients:

_____ _____

_____ _____

_____ _____

_____ _____

_____ _____

_____ _____

Directions:

_____

_____

_____

_____

_____

_____

_____

_____

_____

_____

_____

_____

_____

_____

Notes:

_____

_____

_____

Recipe: _____

Star Rating: ☆ ☆ ☆ ☆ ☆

Prep Time: _____

Cook Time: _____

Oven Temp: _____

Calories: _____

Recipe Nº: _____

Source: _____

Yeild: _____

Serves: _____

Ingredients:

_____   _____

_____   _____

_____   _____

_____   _____

_____   _____

_____   _____

Directions:

_____

_____

_____

_____

_____

_____

_____

_____

_____

_____

_____

Notes:

_____

_____

_____

Recipe: _____

Star Rating: ☆ ☆ ☆ ☆ ☆

Prep Time: _____

Cook Time: _____

Oven Temp: _____

Calories: _____

Recipe Nº: _____

Source: _____

yeild: _____

Serves: _____

Ingredients:

_____ _____ _____ _____

_____ _____ _____ _____

_____ _____ _____ _____

_____ _____ _____ _____

_____ _____ _____ _____

_____ _____ _____ _____

Directions:

_____

_____

_____

_____

_____

_____

_____

_____

_____

_____

_____

_____

_____

_____

Notes:

_____

_____

_____

Recipe: _____

Star Rating: ☆ ☆ ☆ ☆ ☆

Prep Time: _____
Cook Time: _____
Oven Temp: _____
Calories: _____

Recipe N°: _____
Source: _____
Yeild: _____
Serves: _____

Ingredients:

_____ _____
_____ _____
_____ _____
_____ _____
_____ _____
_____ _____

Directions:

_____
_____
_____
_____
_____
_____
_____
_____
_____
_____
_____
_____
_____

Notes:

_____
_____
_____

Recipe: _____

Star Rating: ☆ ☆ ☆ ☆ ☆

Prep Time: _____

Cook Time: _____

Oven Temp: _____

Calories: _____

Recipe N°: _____

Source: _____

Yeild: _____

Serves: _____

Ingredients:

_____ _____   _____ _____
_____ _____   _____ _____
_____ _____   _____ _____
_____ _____   _____ _____
_____ _____   _____ _____
_____ _____   _____ _____

Directions:

_____
_____
_____
_____
_____
_____
_____
_____
_____
_____
_____
_____
_____

Notes:

_____
_____
_____

Recipe: _____

Star Rating: ☆ ☆ ☆ ☆ ☆

- ⏱ Prep Time: _____
- 🍲 Cook Time: _____
- 🔥 Oven Temp: _____
- 🧮 Calories: _____

- \# Recipe Nº: _____
- ⓘ Source: _____
- 🥛 Yeild: _____
- 🍽 Serves: _____

Ingredients

_____   _____

_____   _____

_____   _____

_____   _____

_____   _____

Directions

_____

_____

_____

_____

_____

_____

_____

_____

_____

_____

_____

Notes

_____

_____

_____

Recipe: _____

Star Rating: ☆ ☆ ☆ ☆ ☆

Prep Time: _____

Cook Time: _____

Oven Temp: _____

Calories: _____

Recipe N°: _____

Source: _____

Yeild: _____

Serves: _____

Ingredients:

_____ _____

_____ _____

_____ _____

_____ _____

_____ _____

_____ _____

Directions:

_____

_____

_____

_____

_____

_____

_____

_____

_____

_____

_____

_____

_____

_____

Notes:

_____

_____

_____

Recipe: _____

Star Rating: ☆ ☆ ☆ ☆ ☆

Prep Time: _____

Cook Time: _____

Oven Temp: _____

Calories: _____

Recipe N°: _____

Source: _____

Yeild: _____

Serves: _____

Ingredients

_____ _____
_____ _____
_____ _____
_____ _____
_____ _____

Directions

_____
_____
_____
_____
_____
_____
_____
_____
_____
_____
_____
_____

Notes

_____
_____
_____

Recipe: _____

Star Rating: ☆ ☆ ☆ ☆ ☆

Prep Time: _____

Cook Time: _____

Oven Temp: _____

Calories: _____

Recipe N°: _____

Source: _____

Yeild: _____

Serves: _____

Ingredients:

_____ _____ _____ _____

_____ _____ _____ _____

_____ _____ _____ _____

_____ _____ _____ _____

_____ _____ _____ _____

_____ _____ _____ _____

_____ _____ _____ _____

Directions:

_____

_____

_____

_____

_____

_____

_____

_____

_____

_____

_____

_____

_____

_____

_____

Notes:

_____

_____

_____

Recipe: _____

Star Rating: ☆ ☆ ☆ ☆ ☆

Prep Time: _____
Cook Time: _____
Oven Temp: _____
Calories: _____

Recipe N°: _____
Source: _____
Yeild: _____
Serves: _____

Ingredients:

_____ _____
_____ _____
_____ _____
_____ _____
_____ _____
_____ _____

Directions:

_____
_____
_____
_____
_____
_____
_____
_____
_____
_____
_____
_____
_____

Notes:

_____
_____
_____

Recipe: _____

Star Rating: ☆ ☆ ☆ ☆ ☆

Prep Time: _____

Cook Time: _____

Oven Temp: _____

Calories: _____

Recipe N°: _____

Source: _____

Yeild: _____

Serves: _____

Ingredients:

_____ _____

_____ _____

_____ _____

_____ _____

_____ _____

_____ _____

_____ _____

Directions:

_____

_____

_____

_____

_____

_____

_____

_____

_____

_____

_____

_____

_____

_____

Notes:

_____

_____

_____

_____

Recipe: _____

Star Rating: ☆ ☆ ☆ ☆ ☆

Prep Time: _____

Cook Time: _____

Oven Temp: _____

Calories: _____

Recipe N°: _____

Source: _____

Yeild: _____

Serves: _____

Ingredients:

_____ _____

_____ _____

_____ _____

_____ _____

_____ _____

_____ _____

Directions:

_____

_____

_____

_____

_____

_____

_____

_____

_____

_____

_____

_____

Notes:

_____

_____

_____

Recipe: _____

Star Rating: ☆ ☆ ☆ ☆ ☆

Prep Time: _____

Cook Time: _____

Oven Temp: _____

Calories: _____

Recipe N°: _____

Source: _____

Yeild: _____

Serves: _____

Ingredients:

_____ _____ _____ _____

_____ _____ _____ _____

_____ _____ _____ _____

_____ _____ _____ _____

_____ _____ _____ _____

_____ _____ _____ _____

Directions:

_____

_____

_____

_____

_____

_____

_____

_____

_____

_____

_____

_____

_____

_____

Notes:

_____

_____

_____

Recipe: _____

Star Rating: ☆ ☆ ☆ ☆ ☆

Prep Time: _____

Cook Time: _____

Oven Temp: _____

Calories: _____

Recipe N°: _____

Source: _____

Yeild: _____

Serves: _____

Ingredients:

_____ _____

_____ _____

_____ _____

_____ _____

_____ _____

_____ _____

Directions:

_____

_____

_____

_____

_____

_____

_____

_____

_____

_____

_____

_____

_____

Notes:

_____

_____

_____

_____

Recipe: _____

Star Rating: ☆ ☆ ☆ ☆ ☆

Prep Time: _____

Cook Time: _____

Oven Temp: _____

Calories: _____

Recipe N°: _____

Source: _____

Yeild: _____

Serves: _____

Ingredients:

_____ _____   _____ _____

_____ _____   _____ _____

_____ _____   _____ _____

_____ _____   _____ _____

_____ _____   _____ _____

Directions:

_____

_____

_____

_____

_____

_____

_____

_____

_____

_____

_____

_____

_____

Notes:

_____

_____

_____

Recipe: _____

Star Rating: ☆ ☆ ☆ ☆ ☆

Prep Time: _____

Cook Time: _____

Oven Temp: _____

Calories: _____

Recipe N°: _____

Source: _____

Yeild: _____

Serves: _____

Ingredients:

_____ _____
_____ _____
_____ _____
_____ _____
_____ _____
_____ _____

Directions:

_____
_____
_____
_____
_____
_____
_____
_____
_____
_____
_____
_____
_____

Notes:

_____
_____
_____

Recipe: _____

Star Rating: ☆ ☆ ☆ ☆ ☆

Prep Time: _____

Cook Time: _____

Oven Temp: _____

Calories: _____

Recipe N°: _____

Source: _____

Yeild: _____

Serves: _____

Ingredients:

_____ _____

_____ _____

_____ _____

_____ _____

_____ _____

_____ _____

_____ _____

_____ _____

Directions:

_____

_____

_____

_____

_____

_____

_____

_____

_____

_____

_____

_____

_____

_____

_____

_____

Notes:

_____

_____

_____

Recipe: _____

Star Rating: ☆ ☆ ☆ ☆ ☆

Prep Time: _____
Cook Time: _____
Oven Temp: _____
Calories: _____

Recipe N°: _____
Source: _____
Yeild: _____
Serves: _____

Ingredients:

_____ _____
_____ _____
_____ _____
_____ _____
_____ _____
_____ _____

Directions:

_____
_____
_____
_____
_____
_____
_____
_____
_____
_____
_____
_____

Notes:

_____
_____
_____

Recipe: _____

Star Rating: ☆ ☆ ☆ ☆ ☆

Prep Time: _____

Cook Time: _____

Oven Temp: _____

Calories: _____

Recipe N°: _____

Source: _____

Yeild: _____

Serves: _____

Ingredients:

_____   _____

_____   _____

_____   _____

_____   _____

_____   _____

_____   _____

_____   _____

Directions:

_____

_____

_____

_____

_____

_____

_____

_____

_____

_____

_____

_____

Notes:

_____

_____

_____

Recipe: _____

Star Rating: ☆ ☆ ☆ ☆ ☆

Prep Time: _____

Cook Time: _____

Oven Temp: _____

Calories: _____

Recipe N°: _____

Source: _____

Yeild: _____

Serves: _____

Ingredients:

_____ _____ _____ _____

_____ _____ _____ _____

_____ _____ _____ _____

_____ _____ _____ _____

_____ _____ _____ _____

Directions:

_____

_____

_____

_____

_____

_____

_____

_____

_____

_____

_____

_____

_____

Notes:

_____

_____

_____

Recipe: _____

Star Rating: ☆ ☆ ☆ ☆ ☆

Prep Time: _____

Cook Time: _____

Oven Temp: _____

Calories: _____

Recipe N°: _____

Source: _____

Yeild: _____

Serves: _____

Ingredients:

_____ _____

_____ _____

_____ _____

_____ _____

_____ _____

_____ _____

Directions:

_____

_____

_____

_____

_____

_____

_____

_____

_____

_____

_____

_____

_____

Notes:

_____

_____

_____

Recipe: _____

Star Rating: ☆ ☆ ☆ ☆ ☆

Prep Time: _____

Cook Time: _____

Oven Temp: _____

Calories: _____

Recipe Nº: _____

Source: _____

Yeild: _____

Serves: _____

Ingredients:

_____   _____

_____   _____

_____   _____

_____   _____

_____   _____

_____   _____

_____   _____

Directions:

_____

_____

_____

_____

_____

_____

_____

_____

_____

_____

_____

_____

Notes:

_____

_____

_____

Recipe: _____

Star Rating: ☆ ☆ ☆ ☆ ☆

Prep Time: _____

Cook Time: _____

Oven Temp: _____

Calories: _____

Recipe N°: _____

Source: _____

yeild: _____

Serves: _____

Ingredients:

_____ _____   _____ _____

_____ _____   _____ _____

_____ _____   _____ _____

_____ _____   _____ _____

_____ _____   _____ _____

Directions:

_____

_____

_____

_____

_____

_____

_____

_____

_____

_____

_____

_____

Notes:

_____

_____

_____

Recipe: _____

Star Rating: ☆ ☆ ☆ ☆ ☆

Prep Time: _____

Cook Time: _____

Oven Temp: _____

Calories: _____

Recipe Nº: _____

Source: _____

Yeild: _____

Serves: _____

Ingredients.

_____ _____

_____ _____

_____ _____

_____ _____

_____ _____

_____ _____

Directions.

_____

_____

_____

_____

_____

_____

_____

_____

_____

_____

_____

Notes.

_____

_____

_____

Recipe: _____

Star Rating: ☆ ☆ ☆ ☆ ☆

Prep Time: _____

Cook Time: _____

Oven Temp: _____

Calories: _____

Recipe N°: _____

Source: _____

Yeild: _____

Serves: _____

Ingredients:

_____ _____ | _____ _____

_____ _____ | _____ _____

_____ _____ | _____ _____

_____ _____ | _____ _____

_____ _____ | _____ _____

_____ _____ | _____ _____

Directions:

_____

_____

_____

_____

_____

_____

_____

_____

_____

_____

_____

_____

_____

Notes:

_____

_____

_____

Recipe: _____

Star Rating: ☆ ☆ ☆ ☆ ☆

- ⏱ Prep Time: _____
- 🍲 Cook Time: _____
- 🔲 Oven Temp: _____
- 🧮 Calories: _____

- # Recipe N°: _____
- ⓘ Source: _____
- 🥡 Yeild: _____
- 🍽 Serves: _____

🥚 Ingredients:

_____ _____ _____ _____
_____ _____ _____ _____
_____ _____ _____ _____
_____ _____ _____ _____
_____ _____ _____ _____
_____ _____ _____ _____

🍳 Directions:

_____
_____
_____
_____
_____
_____
_____
_____
_____
_____
_____
_____
_____
_____

📝 Notes:

_____
_____
_____
_____

Recipe: _____

Star Rating: ☆ ☆ ☆ ☆ ☆

Prep Time: _____
Cook Time: _____
Oven Temp: _____
Calories: _____

Recipe N°: _____
Source: _____
Yeild: _____
Serves: _____

Ingredients:

_____ _____
_____ _____
_____ _____
_____ _____
_____ _____
_____ _____
_____ _____

Directions:

_____
_____
_____
_____
_____
_____
_____
_____
_____
_____
_____
_____
_____
_____
_____
_____

Notes:

_____
_____
_____

Recipe: _____

Star Rating: ☆ ☆ ☆ ☆ ☆

Prep Time: _____

Cook Time: _____

Oven Temp: _____

Calories: _____

Recipe N°: _____

Source: _____

Yeild: _____

Serves: _____

Ingredients:

_____ _____

_____ _____

_____ _____

_____ _____

_____ _____

_____ _____

_____ _____

Directions:

_____

_____

_____

_____

_____

_____

_____

_____

_____

_____

_____

Notes:

_____

_____

_____

Recipe: _____

Star Rating: ☆ ☆ ☆ ☆ ☆

Prep Time: _____

Cook Time: _____

Oven Temp: _____

Calories: _____

Recipe N°: _____

Source: _____

yeild: _____

Serves: _____

Ingredients:

_____   _____

_____   _____

_____   _____

_____   _____

_____   _____

_____   _____

Directions:

_____

_____

_____

_____

_____

_____

_____

_____

_____

_____

_____

_____

_____

Notes:

_____

_____

_____

Recipe: _____

Star Rating: ☆ ☆ ☆ ☆ ☆

🔪🕐 Prep Time: _____   # Recipe N°: _____

🥘🕐 Cook Time: _____   ⓘ Source: _____

🔥🌡 Oven Temp: _____   🥡 Yeild: _____

🧮🍎 Calories: _____   🍽 Serves: _____

🥛 Ingredients:

_____   _____

_____   _____

_____   _____

_____   _____

_____   _____

_____   _____

🥄 Directions:

_____

_____

_____

_____

_____

_____

_____

_____

_____

_____

_____

_____

_____

📝 Notes:

_____

_____

_____

Recipe: _____

Star Rating: ☆ ☆ ☆ ☆ ☆

Prep Time: _____

Cook Time: _____

Oven Temp: _____

Calories: _____

Recipe Nº: _____

Source: _____

Yeild: _____

Serves: _____

Ingredients:

_____ _____
_____ _____
_____ _____
_____ _____
_____ _____
_____ _____

Directions:

_____
_____
_____
_____
_____
_____
_____
_____
_____
_____
_____
_____
_____
_____

Notes.

_____
_____
_____

Recipe: _____

Star Rating: ☆ ☆ ☆ ☆ ☆

Prep Time: _____
Cook Time: _____
Oven Temp: _____
Calories: _____

Recipe N°: _____
Source: _____
Yeild: _____
Serves: _____

Ingredients.

_____ _____
_____ _____
_____ _____
_____ _____
_____ _____
_____ _____

Directions.

_____
_____
_____
_____
_____
_____
_____
_____
_____
_____
_____

Notes.

_____
_____
_____

Recipe: _____

Star Rating: ☆ ☆ ☆ ☆ ☆

Prep Time: _____

Cook Time: _____

Oven Temp: _____

Calories: _____

Recipe N°: _____

Source: _____

Yeild: _____

Serves: _____

Ingredients:

_____   _____   _____   _____

_____   _____   _____   _____

_____   _____   _____   _____

_____   _____   _____   _____

_____   _____   _____   _____

_____   _____   _____   _____

Directions:

_____

_____

_____

_____

_____

_____

_____

_____

_____

_____

_____

_____

_____

_____

_____

_____

Notes:

_____

_____

_____

Recipe: _____

Star Rating: ☆ ☆ ☆ ☆ ☆

🕐 Prep Time: _____
🍲 Cook Time: _____
🔲 Oven Temp: _____
🔢 Calories: _____

\# Recipe N°: _____
ⓘ Source: _____
🥛 Yeild: _____
🍽 Serves: _____

Ingredients.

_____   _____
_____   _____
_____   _____
_____   _____
_____   _____
_____   _____

Directions.

_____
_____
_____
_____
_____
_____
_____
_____
_____
_____
_____

Notes.

_____
_____
_____

Recipe: _____

Star Rating: ☆ ☆ ☆ ☆ ☆

Prep Time: _____

Cook Time: _____

Oven Temp: _____

Calories: _____

Recipe N°: _____

Source: _____

Yeild: _____

Serves: _____

Ingredients:

_____   _____

_____   _____

_____   _____

_____   _____

_____   _____

_____   _____

Directions:

_____

_____

_____

_____

_____

_____

_____

_____

_____

_____

_____

_____

Notes:

_____

_____

_____

Recipe: _____

Star Rating: ☆ ☆ ☆ ☆ ☆

Prep Time. _____

Cook Time. _____

Oven Temp. _____

Calories: _____

Recipe N°: _____

Source: _____

Yeild: _____

Serves: _____

Ingredients.

_____ _____

_____ _____

_____ _____

_____ _____

_____ _____

_____ _____

Directions.

_____

_____

_____

_____

_____

_____

_____

_____

_____

_____

_____

_____

Notes.

_____

_____

_____

_____

Recipe: _____

Star Rating: ☆ ☆ ☆ ☆ ☆

Prep Time: _____

Cook Time: _____

Oven Temp: _____

Calories: _____

Recipe N°: _____

Source: _____

Yeild: _____

Serves: _____

Ingredients:

_____ _____   _____ _____

_____ _____   _____ _____

_____ _____   _____ _____

_____ _____   _____ _____

_____ _____   _____ _____

_____ _____   _____ _____

Directions:

_____

_____

_____

_____

_____

_____

_____

_____

_____

_____

_____

_____

_____

_____

Notes:

_____

_____

_____

Recipe:

Star Rating: ☆ ☆ ☆ ☆ ☆

Prep Time: _____

Cook Time: _____

Oven Temp: _____

Calories: _____

Recipe N°: _____

Source: _____

Yeild: _____

Serves: _____

Ingredients:

_____ _____
_____ _____
_____ _____
_____ _____
_____ _____
_____ _____

Directions:

_____
_____
_____
_____
_____
_____
_____
_____
_____
_____
_____
_____

Notes:

_____
_____
_____

Recipe: _____

Star Rating: ☆ ☆ ☆ ☆ ☆

Prep Time: _____

Cook Time: _____

Oven Temp: _____

Calories: _____

Recipe N°: _____

Source: _____

Yeild: _____

Serves: _____

Ingredients:

_____ _____
_____ _____
_____ _____
_____ _____
_____ _____
_____ _____
_____ _____

Directions:

_____
_____
_____
_____
_____
_____
_____
_____
_____
_____
_____
_____
_____
_____

Notes:

_____
_____
_____

Recipe: _____

Star Rating: ☆ ☆ ☆ ☆ ☆

Prep Time: _____

Cook Time: _____

Oven Temp: _____

Calories: _____

Recipe N°: _____

Source: _____

Yeild: _____

Serves: _____

Ingredients:

_____　_____

_____　_____

_____　_____

_____　_____

_____　_____

_____　_____

Directions:

_____

_____

_____

_____

_____

_____

_____

_____

_____

_____

_____

_____

Notes:

_____

_____

_____

Recipe: _____

Star Rating: ☆ ☆ ☆ ☆ ☆

Prep Time: _____

Cook Time: _____

Oven Temp: _____

Calories: _____

Recipe N°: _____

Source: _____

yeild: _____

Serves: _____

Ingredients:

_____   _____
_____   _____
_____   _____
_____   _____
_____   _____
_____   _____

Directions:

_____
_____
_____
_____
_____
_____
_____
_____
_____
_____
_____
_____

Notes:

_____
_____
_____

Recipe: _____

Star Rating: ☆ ☆ ☆ ☆ ☆

Prep Time: _____

Cook Time: _____

Oven Temp: _____

Calories: _____

\# Recipe N°: _____

Source: _____

Yeild: _____

Serves: _____

Ingredients:

_____ _____

_____ _____

_____ _____

_____ _____

_____ _____

_____ _____

Directions:

_____

_____

_____

_____

_____

_____

_____

_____

_____

_____

_____

_____

Notes:

_____

_____

_____

Recipe: _____

Star Rating: ☆ ☆ ☆ ☆ ☆

Prep Time: _____

Cook Time: _____

Oven Temp: _____

Calories: _____

Recipe N°: _____

Source: _____

Yeild: _____

Serves: _____

Ingredients:

_____ _____

_____ _____

_____ _____

_____ _____

_____ _____

_____ _____

Directions:

_____

_____

_____

_____

_____

_____

_____

_____

_____

_____

_____

_____

_____

Notes:

_____

_____

_____

Recipe:

Star Rating: ☆ ☆ ☆ ☆ ☆

Prep Time: _____

Cook Time: _____

Oven Temp: _____

Calories: _____

Recipe Nº: _____

Source: _____

Yeild: _____

Serves: _____

Ingredients:

Directions:

Notes:

Recipe: _____

Star Rating: ☆ ☆ ☆ ☆ ☆

Prep Time: _____

Cook Time: _____

Oven Temp: _____

Calories: _____

Recipe N°: _____

Source: _____

yeild: _____

Serves: _____

Ingredients:

_____   _____
_____   _____
_____   _____
_____   _____
_____   _____
_____   _____
_____   _____

Directions:

_____
_____
_____
_____
_____
_____
_____
_____
_____
_____
_____
_____
_____
_____

Notes:

_____
_____
_____

Recipe: _____

Star Rating: ☆ ☆ ☆ ☆ ☆

Prep Time: _____

Cook Time: _____

Oven Temp: _____

Calories: _____

Recipe N°: _____

Source: _____

Yeild: _____

Serves: _____

Ingredients:

_____ _____
_____ _____
_____ _____
_____ _____
_____ _____
_____ _____

Directions:

_____
_____
_____
_____
_____
_____
_____
_____
_____
_____
_____
_____

Notes:

_____
_____
_____

Recipe: _____

Star Rating: ☆ ☆ ☆ ☆ ☆

Prep Time: _____

Cook Time: _____

Oven Temp: _____

Calories: _____

Recipe N°: _____

Source: _____

Yeild: _____

Serves: _____

Ingredients.

_____ _____

_____ _____

_____ _____

_____ _____

_____ _____

_____ _____

_____ _____

Directions.

_____

_____

_____

_____

_____

_____

_____

_____

_____

_____

_____

_____

_____

Notes.

_____

_____

_____

Recipe: _____

Star Rating: ☆ ☆ ☆ ☆ ☆

Prep Time: _____

Cook Time: _____

Oven Temp: _____

Calories: _____

Recipe N°: _____

Source: _____

Yeild: _____

Serves: _____

Ingredients.

_____ _____

_____ _____

_____ _____

_____ _____

_____ _____

Directions.

_____

_____

_____

_____

_____

_____

_____

_____

_____

_____

_____

_____

Notes.

_____

_____

_____

Recipe: _____

Star Rating: ☆ ☆ ☆ ☆ ☆

Prep Time: _____

Cook Time: _____

Oven Temp: _____

Calories: _____

Recipe Nº: _____

Source: _____

Yeild: _____

Serves: _____

Ingredients:

_____ _____   _____ _____

_____ _____   _____ _____

_____ _____   _____ _____

_____ _____   _____ _____

_____ _____   _____ _____

_____ _____   _____ _____

Directions:

_____

_____

_____

_____

_____

_____

_____

_____

_____

_____

_____

_____

_____

_____

Notes:

_____

_____

_____

Recipe: _____

Star Rating: ☆ ☆ ☆ ☆ ☆

Prep Time: _____

Cook Time: _____

Oven Temp: _____

Calories: _____

Recipe Nº: _____

Source: _____

yeild: _____

Serves: _____

Ingredients:

_____ _____

_____ _____

_____ _____

_____ _____

_____ _____

_____ _____

Directions:

_____

_____

_____

_____

_____

_____

_____

_____

_____

_____

_____

_____

Notes:

_____

_____

_____

Recipe: _____

Star Rating: ☆ ☆ ☆ ☆ ☆

Prep Time: _____

Cook Time: _____

Oven Temp: _____

Calories: _____

Recipe N°: _____

Source: _____

Yeild: _____

Serves: _____

Ingredients:

_____ _____
_____ _____
_____ _____
_____ _____
_____ _____
_____ _____
_____ _____

Directions:

_____
_____
_____
_____
_____
_____
_____
_____
_____
_____
_____
_____
_____
_____

Notes:

_____
_____
_____

Recipe: _____

Star Rating: ☆ ☆ ☆ ☆ ☆

Prep Time: _____

Cook Time: _____

Oven Temp: _____

Calories: _____

Recipe N°: _____

Source: _____

Yeild: _____

Serves: _____

Ingredients:

_____   _____

_____   _____

_____   _____

_____   _____

_____   _____

Directions:

_____

_____

_____

_____

_____

_____

_____

_____

_____

_____

_____

Notes:

_____

_____

_____

Recipe:

Star Rating: ☆ ☆ ☆ ☆ ☆

Prep Time: _____

Cook Time: _____

Oven Temp: _____

Calories: _____

Recipe N°: _____

Source: _____

Yeild: _____

Serves: _____

Ingredients:

_____ _____   _____ _____

_____ _____   _____ _____

_____ _____   _____ _____

_____ _____   _____ _____

_____ _____   _____ _____

_____ _____   _____ _____

Directions:

_____

_____

_____

_____

_____

_____

_____

_____

_____

_____

_____

_____

Notes:

_____

_____

_____

Recipe: _____

Star Rating: ☆ ☆ ☆ ☆ ☆

Prep Time: _____

Cook Time: _____

Oven Temp: _____

Calories: _____

Recipe N°: _____

Source: _____

Yeild: _____

Serves: _____

Ingredients:

_____ _____   _____ _____

_____ _____   _____ _____

_____ _____   _____ _____

_____ _____   _____ _____

_____ _____   _____ _____

_____ _____   _____ _____

Directions:

_____

_____

_____

_____

_____

_____

_____

_____

_____

_____

_____

_____

_____

_____

Notes:

_____

_____

_____

_____

Recipe:

Star Rating: ☆ ☆ ☆ ☆ ☆

Prep Time:

Cook Time:

Oven Temp:

Calories:

Recipe N°:

Source:

yeild.

Serves:

Ingredients.

Directions.

Notes.

Recipe: _____

Star Rating: ☆ ☆ ☆ ☆ ☆

Prep Time: _____

Cook Time: _____

Oven Temp: _____

Calories: _____

Recipe N°: _____

Source: _____

Yeild: _____

Serves: _____

Ingredients:

_____ _____

_____ _____

_____ _____

_____ _____

_____ _____

_____ _____

Directions:

Notes:

Recipe: _____

Star Rating: ☆ ☆ ☆ ☆ ☆

Prep Time: _____

Cook Time: _____

Oven Temp: _____

Calories: _____

Recipe N°: _____

Source: _____

Yeild: _____

Serves: _____

Ingredients:

_____ _____

_____ _____

_____ _____

_____ _____

_____ _____

_____ _____

Directions:

_____

_____

_____

_____

_____

_____

_____

_____

_____

_____

_____

_____

_____

_____

Notes:

_____

_____

_____

Recipe: _____

Star Rating: ☆ ☆ ☆ ☆ ☆

Prep Time: _____

Cook Time: _____

Oven Temp: _____

Calories: _____

Recipe N°: _____

Source: _____

yeild: _____

Serves: _____

Ingredients.

_____ _____

_____ _____

_____ _____

_____ _____

_____ _____

_____ _____

Directions.

_____

_____

_____

_____

_____

_____

_____

_____

_____

_____

_____

_____

Notes.

_____

_____

_____

Recipe: _____

Star Rating: ☆ ☆ ☆ ☆ ☆

Prep Time: _____

Cook Time: _____

Oven Temp: _____

Calories: _____

Recipe N°: _____

Source: _____

Yeild: _____

Serves: _____

Ingredients:

_____ _____

_____ _____

_____ _____

_____ _____

_____ _____

_____ _____

_____ _____

Directions:

_____

_____

_____

_____

_____

_____

_____

_____

_____

_____

_____

_____

_____

_____

_____

Notes:

_____

_____

_____

Recipe: _____

Star Rating: ☆ ☆ ☆ ☆ ☆

Prep Time: _____

Cook Time: _____

Oven Temp: _____

Calories: _____

Recipe n°: _____

Source: _____

Yeild: _____

Serves: _____

Ingredients.

_____ _____
_____ _____
_____ _____
_____ _____
_____ _____
_____ _____

Directions.

_____
_____
_____
_____
_____
_____
_____
_____
_____
_____
_____
_____

Notes.

_____
_____
_____

Recipe: _____

Star Rating: ☆ ☆ ☆ ☆ ☆

Prep Time: _____

Cook Time: _____

Oven Temp: _____

Calories: _____

Recipe N°: _____

Source: _____

Yeild: _____

Serves: _____

Ingredients:

_____   _____
_____   _____
_____   _____
_____   _____
_____   _____
_____   _____
_____   _____

Directions:

_____
_____
_____
_____
_____
_____
_____
_____
_____
_____
_____
_____
_____
_____
_____

Notes:

_____
_____
_____

Recipe: _____

Star Rating: ☆ ☆ ☆ ☆ ☆

Prep Time: _____

Cook Time: _____

Oven Temp: _____

Calories: _____

Recipe N°: _____

Source: _____

Yeild: _____

Serves: _____

Ingredients:

_____ _____

_____ _____

_____ _____

_____ _____

_____ _____

_____ _____

_____ _____

Directions:

_____

_____

_____

_____

_____

_____

_____

_____

_____

_____

_____

_____

_____

Notes:

_____

_____

_____

Recipe: _____

Star Rating: ☆ ☆ ☆ ☆ ☆

Prep Time: _____

Cook Time: _____

Oven Temp: _____

Calories: _____

Recipe Nº: _____

Source: _____

Yeild: _____

Serves: _____

Ingredients:

_____ _____ _____ _____
_____ _____ _____ _____
_____ _____ _____ _____
_____ _____ _____ _____
_____ _____ _____ _____
_____ _____ _____ _____

Directions:

_____
_____
_____
_____
_____
_____
_____
_____
_____
_____
_____
_____
_____
_____

Notes:

_____
_____
_____

Recipe: _____

Star Rating: ☆ ☆ ☆ ☆ ☆

Prep Time. _____

Cook Time. _____

Oven Temp. _____

Calories. _____

Recipe N°: _____

Source. _____

Yeild. _____

Serves. _____

Ingredients.

_____ _____ _____ _____

_____ _____ _____ _____

_____ _____ _____ _____

_____ _____ _____ _____

_____ _____ _____ _____

Directions.

_____

_____

_____

_____

_____

_____

_____

_____

_____

_____

_____

_____

_____

_____

_____

Notes.

_____

_____

_____

Recipe: _____

Star Rating: ☆ ☆ ☆ ☆ ☆

Prep Time: _____

Cook Time: _____

Oven Temp: _____

Calories: _____

Recipe N°: _____

Source: _____

Yeild: _____

Serves: _____

Ingredients.

_____ _____ _____ _____
_____ _____ _____ _____
_____ _____ _____ _____
_____ _____ _____ _____
_____ _____ _____ _____
_____ _____ _____ _____

Directions.

_____
_____
_____
_____
_____
_____
_____
_____
_____
_____
_____
_____
_____
_____

Notes.

_____
_____
_____

Recipe:

Star Rating: ☆ ☆ ☆ ☆ ☆

- Prep Time:
- Cook Time:
- Oven Temp:
- Calories:

- Recipe N°:
- Source:
- Yeild:
- Serves:

Ingredients:

Directions:

Notes:

Recipe: _____

Star Rating: ☆ ☆ ☆ ☆ ☆

Prep Time: _____

Cook Time: _____

Oven Temp: _____

Calories: _____

Recipe N°: _____

Source: _____

yeild: _____

Serves: _____

Ingredients:

_____ _____ _____ _____

_____ _____ _____ _____

_____ _____ _____ _____

_____ _____ _____ _____

_____ _____ _____ _____

_____ _____ _____ _____

_____ _____ _____ _____

Directions:

_____

_____

_____

_____

_____

_____

_____

_____

_____

_____

_____

_____

_____

_____

_____

_____

Notes:

_____

_____

_____

_____

Recipe: _____

Star Rating: ☆ ☆ ☆ ☆ ☆

Prep Time: _____

Cook Time: _____

Oven Temp: _____

Calories: _____

Recipe N°: _____

Source: _____

Yeild: _____

Serves: _____

Ingredients:

_____   _____
_____   _____
_____   _____
_____   _____
_____   _____
_____   _____

Directions:

_____
_____
_____
_____
_____
_____
_____
_____
_____
_____
_____
_____

Notes:

_____
_____
_____

Recipe: _____

Star Rating: ☆ ☆ ☆ ☆ ☆

Prep Time: _____

Cook Time: _____

Oven Temp: _____

Calories: _____

Recipe N°: _____

Source: _____

Yeild: _____

Serves: _____

Ingredients:

_____ _____   _____ _____

_____ _____   _____ _____

_____ _____   _____ _____

_____ _____   _____ _____

_____ _____   _____ _____

_____ _____   _____ _____

Directions:

_____

_____

_____

_____

_____

_____

_____

_____

_____

_____

_____

_____

_____

_____

Notes:

_____

_____

_____

Recipe: _____

Star Rating: ☆ ☆ ☆ ☆ ☆

Prep Time: _____

Cook Time: _____

Oven Temp: _____

Calories: _____

Recipe N°: _____

Source: _____

Yeild: _____

Serves: _____

Ingredients:

_____ _____

_____ _____

_____ _____

_____ _____

_____ _____

_____ _____

Directions:

_____

_____

_____

_____

_____

_____

_____

_____

_____

_____

_____

_____

_____

_____

Notes:

_____

_____

_____

Recipe: _____

Star Rating: ☆ ☆ ☆ ☆ ☆

Prep Time: _____

Cook Time: _____

Oven Temp: _____

Calories: _____

Recipe N°: _____

Source: _____

Yeild: _____

Serves: _____

Ingredients:

_____ _____ _____ _____

_____ _____ _____ _____

_____ _____ _____ _____

_____ _____ _____ _____

_____ _____ _____ _____

Directions:

_____

_____

_____

_____

_____

_____

_____

_____

_____

_____

_____

_____

_____

Notes:

_____

_____

_____

Notes:

Notes:

Notes:

Notes:

Notes:

Notes:

Printed in Great Britain
by Amazon

33958688R00093